2103

SLOUGH TO NEWBURY

Vic Mitchell and Keith Smith

MP Middleton Press

Cover picture: Newbury Racecourse once generated much extra traffic on the route. No. 5074 **Hampden** *and no. 6010* **King Charles I** *have just arrived with racegoers on 5th March 1960. (R.C.Riley)*

First published November 2000

ISBN 1 901706 56 7

© *Middleton Press, 2000*

Design Deborah Esher

Published by
        Middleton Press
        Easebourne Lane
        Midhurst, West Sussex
        GU29 9AZ
Tel: 01730 813169
Fax: 01730 812601

Printed & bound by Biddles Ltd,
        Guildford and Kings Lynn

INDEX

Railway Clearing House map for 1947 with Southern Railway lines
solid and GWR routes hollow.

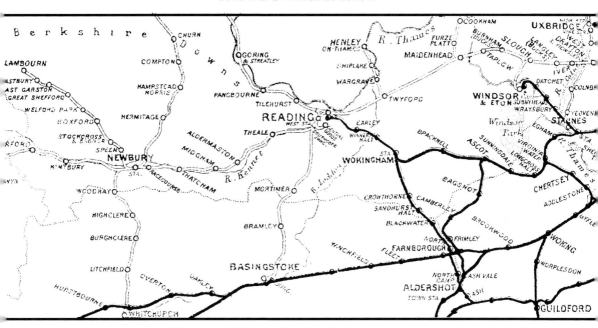

ACKNOWLEDGEMENTS

We are very grateful for the help received from so many of the photographers. Our thanks also go to R.S.Carpenter, G.Croughton, N.Langridge, D.Trevor Rowe, Mr D. and Dr S.Salter, E.Youldon and our ever supportive wives.

GEOGRAPHICAL SETTING

Slough to Reading

This section is in the Thames Valley, but is several miles south of the river between Maidenhead and Taplow. Nevertheless, Brunel was able to engineer the line to have a steady rising gradient no steeper than 1 in 1320 by creating an embankment across the Loddon Valley and a deep cutting at Sonning, both west of Twyford. However, its depth has been reduced subsequently. The subsoil is gravel and clay.

Reading to Newbury

The line is entirely within the Kennet Valley, the river joining the Thames east of Reading. The railway, the River Kennet and the Kennet & Avon Canal run in close proximity all the way to Newbury.

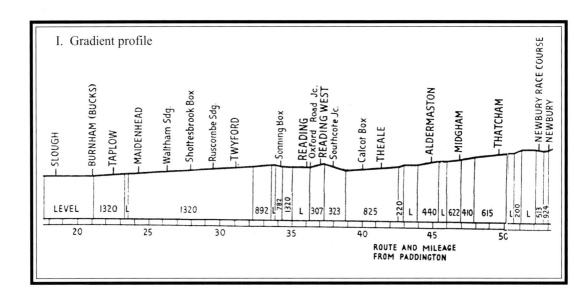

I. Gradient profile

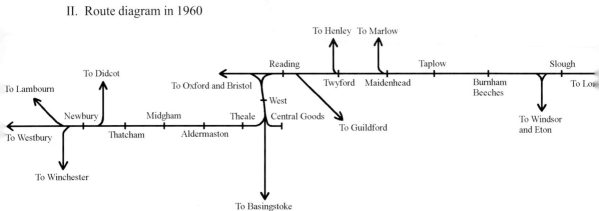

II. Route diagram in 1960

HISTORICAL BACKGROUND

The Great Western Railway from London opened in stages: to Maidenhead on 4th June 1838 (to a station east of the river), to Twyford on 1st July 1839, to Reading on 3rd March 1840 and on to Didcot, Chippenham and Bath in 1841. Most of the route had been authorised under an Act dated 31st August 1835. Its engineer was I.K.Brunel.

The Berks & Hants Railway of the GWR received its Act in 1845 and trains between Reading and Hungerford commenced on 21st December 1847. The route featured in this album became part of the main line to Bath and Weymouth in 1862.

Branches were opened thus: to Basingstoke in 1848, to Windsor in 1849, to High Wycombe in 1853, to Henley-on-Thames in 1857 and to Reading Central Goods in 1908. The only competing line in the area was that of the South Eastern Railway, which reached Reading in 1849. Much later, other lines reached Newbury: from Didcot in 1882, from Winchester in 1885 and from Lambourn in 1898.

Earlier competition had been provided by the Kennet & Avon Canal, which had opened from Reading to Newbury in 1723 and through to Bristol in 1810. It was bought by the GWR in 1857.

The GWR lines were laid to the broad gauge of 7ft 0¼ins, despite its neighbours using standard gauge. To permit through running of freight between the Midlands and the South of England, a third rail was added on the tracks north from Basingstoke to Oxford and used from 22nd December 1857. Mixed gauge was available through Reading station from 1st December 1858, this allowing goods traffic to run between the SER and Oxford. The east side of the triangular junction and the route to Paddington could be used by standard gauge trains from 1st October 1861. The last broad gauge train ran on 21st May 1892.

The quadrupling of the tracks between Slough and Taplow was completed on 8th September 1884, but this did not reach Reading until 4th June 1893.

There were no major changes until the GWR was nationalised in 1948, to become the Western Region of British Railways, when the visible changes were few. Trains began to appear in sector liveries - InterCity and Network SouthEast - in the mid-1980s - these being followed in the mid-1990s by Thames Trains and Great Western Trains colours as a prelude to privatisation. The former franchise was let on 13th October 1996 and the latter on 4th February of the same year; the owning companies became Victory Railway Holdings and First Group respectively.

PASSENGER SERVICES

Slough to Reading

The first timetable showed eight weekday and six Sunday trains, but reliability was poor. In 1850, there were ten trains to Reading and an additional three as far as Maidenhead. On Sundays, there were five to Reading.

The 1870 timetable showed 20 down arrivals, six of which were non-stop from Paddington, most having slip coaches for some intermediate stations. There were six Sunday trains.

Twenty years later, there were 28 weekday trains with a complex stopping pattern, but there were only seven Sunday trains. The frequency increased steadily, always giving Reading one of the best train services in the Home Counties.

Reading to Newbury

Below is a summary of down train frequencies.

	Weekdays	Sundays
1850	4	2
1870	5	2
1890	7	2
1910	18	2

The nineteenth century trains listed above called at all intermediate stations on the route. The twentieth century saw a steady improvement in the service, except during the two World Wars, and many ran fast between Reading and Newbury.

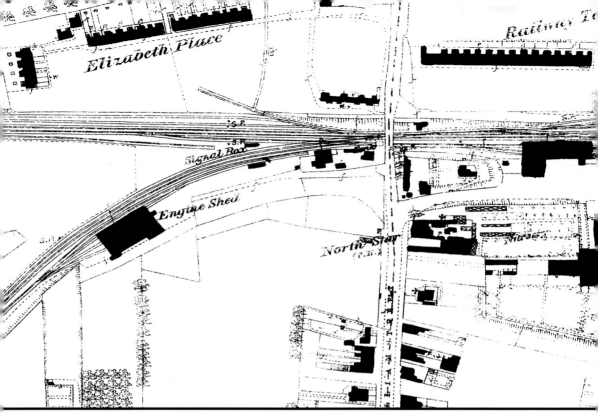

Map labels: Elizabeth Place · Railwa... · Signal Box · Engine Shed · North Star (P.H.) · House · Signal Box

III.   The first edition from about 1870 shows two separate stations for up and down trains but both on the down side. This arrangement was common in the early years of the GWR at important stations, the next example westwards being at Reading. Between the two buildings are two short sidings radiating from a turntable; they were used for wagons bearing horse-drawn carriages. The siding at the top of the right page ran to a corn mill. The lower line at the right border served a brick works. The Windsor branch is lower left, it being part of a triangular junction.

1.   London-bound passengers used the building on the left, the carriages of the wealthy being loaded in the foreground. Note its similarity to the one existing at Reading. The Royal Hotel (right) was rather grander than the station and is shown on the join in the map. The opening of the station was delayed until 4th June 1841, owing to objections by Eton College. It seems that there was a fear that a railway might encourage inmates to abscond. (British Rail)

SLOUGH

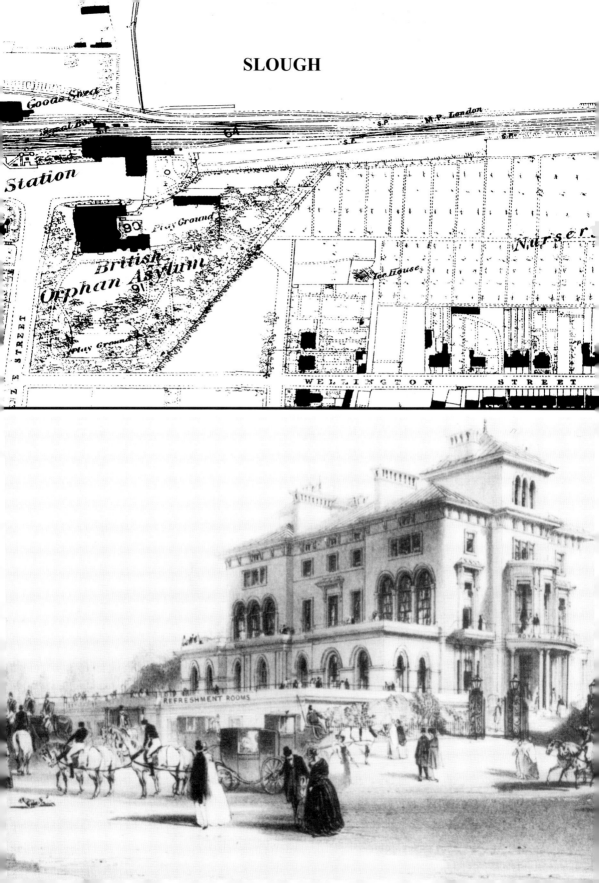

2. This westward view is probably from the 1890s, before a third track was laid between the two relief lines (right) and East Box was erected on the site of the bay in the centre of the picture. The perforated signals are for shunting movements. Records suggest that trains stopped here unofficially from the outset and that someone from Eton College even requested a special train to run on 28th June 1838. (LPC/NRM)

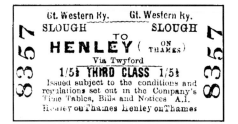

3. The 6100 class was introduced in 1931 and one is seen on a down local train in that decade, passing Windsor Branch Junction Box. This had 101 levers and was still controlling signals on tapered wooden posts. (Lens of Sutton)

4.　　A broken rail west of the station on 1st May 1959 caused the derailment of the rear six coaches of the up "Pembroke Coast Express". The rest of the train passed through the station, with the restaurant car off the rails. It can be seen in picture 119 in *Ealing to Slough*. (F.Hornby)

5.　　Another westward view includes no. 6932 *Burwarton Hall* on the down relief line in June 1952. The cattle dock is beyond the horseboxes and West Yard is beyond the bridge. The centre bay (right) was in use until 1961 and had been used by a local service to Slough Trading Estate in earlier years. (D.B.Clayton)

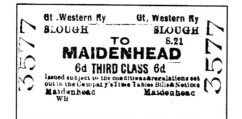

6.　　The three-road engine shed shown on the map gained a fourth line in 1872. It had a fifth line added, in about 1935, under the lean-to seen to the left of 0-4-2T no. 1453 on 5th March 1961. The locomotives are on the "Fitter's Road", the only one that did not run through the shed. The 45ft turntable was beyond it. The first shed had a single road and lasted until 1868. Its successor was reroofed in 1954 and closed in 1964. Demolition took place in 1970. (F.Hornby)

7.   The shed (left) had tank engines exclusively after 1940: 48 in 1950, 32 in 1960 and 7 upon closure. In the triangle (centre) are permanent way sidings and a three-road carriage shed, but this is out of view. Two 3-car DMUs approach the up main platform in April 1963. (T.Wright)

8.   Running on the up main line on 10th October 1963 is no. 7035 *Ogmore Castle*, with an express from Worcester. West Box stands at the west end of the triangular Windsor junction. Along with the two other Slough boxes, it closed on 14th October 1963, hence the white cross on the new colour light signal. Built in 1930, the box had 74 levers. (R.C.Riley)

**A later map and other views
of this station can be found in
the companion album,
*Ealing to Slough.***

9.   The down "Bristol Pullman" was recorded from the steps of West Box on the same day. The new panel box (obscured by the second coach) was itself superseded by an IECC (Integrated Electronic Control Centre) in 1993. The line lower right lasted until 1970, but its companion was taken out of use in September 1963. The goods yard (left) had a 6-ton crane and was in use until 6th October 1980. (R.C.Riley)

10.   The Windsor branch train is at platform 1 while the 10.45 Paddington to Cardiff calls at 11.00 on 9th June 1978. Such trains were hourly and called also at Bristol Parkway. HSTs were introduced to the route in 1976 and have served travellers well. (T.Heavyside)

→

11.   From 9th June 1978, a panoramic view of the west end of the station includes the impressive domed roofs on the north side. No. W51333 departs from platform 4, while mail vans stand in the bay later used by tampers. The centre bay has been infilled and the canopies joined together. (T.Heavyside)

12.   The Windsor branch connection is on the left as an up train approaches platform 5 on 23rd June 1990. The front of no. 50036 and the coaches carry the Network SouthEast logos. The up goods loop is behind the train; the lines through platforms 2 and 5 were signalled for reversible running. The building to the right of the fourth and fifth coaches had been the goods shed, the white panel replacing the wagon doorway. (A.Dasi-Sutton)

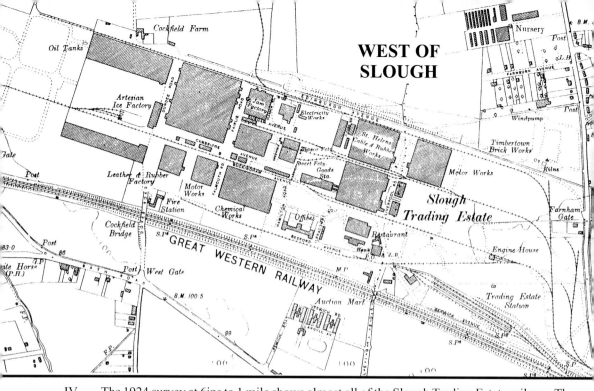

IV. The 1924 survey at 6ins to 1 mile shows almost all of the Slough Trading Estate railway. The area was a WD depot from 1916 until 1920, when development of the Estate began. The passenger station existed until 1956, workmen's trains running to and from Paddington and Slough to serve up to 160 firms on the site. The four platforms were unsurfaced and devoid of seats and shelters, but were electrically lit. There was a wooden footbridge at their east end but only the southern pair was used after 1924. An emergency connection to the nearby Estates siding was added prior to World War II. In 1947 there was one train originating at Slough and one at Paddington, while four returned to the latter at the end of the day, but the service was withdrawn in about 1950.

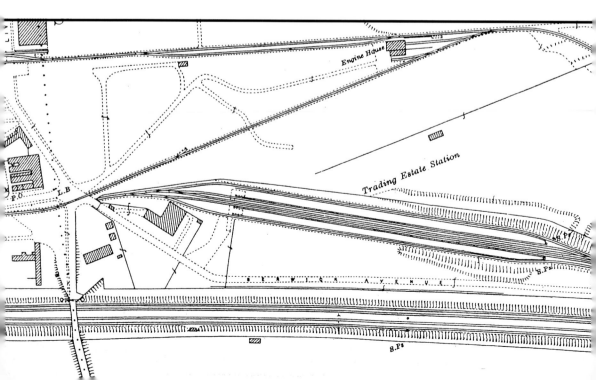

13.　No. 3 was recorded on Buckingham Avenue in 1970. This locomotive came from Hudswell Clarke in 1924 and went to the Mid-Hants Railway in 1973, but was never used on that line although it remained there until 1986. (G.Merrin)

V.　The tracks to the Estate's private station branched from the relief lines, whereas its goods traffic was conveyed via the sidings of West Yard, lower right. The junction was controlled by Farnham Road Box, which had 74 levers and closed on 19th November 1962. One siding remained in use for oil traffic until 27th April 1973. During the life of the Estate system there were five different locomotives, eight wagons and two steam cranes.

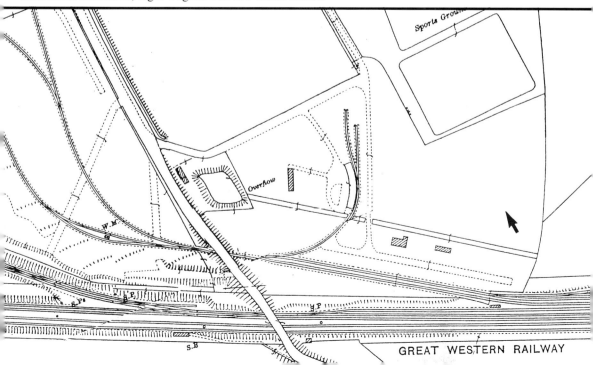

GREAT WESTERN RAILWAY

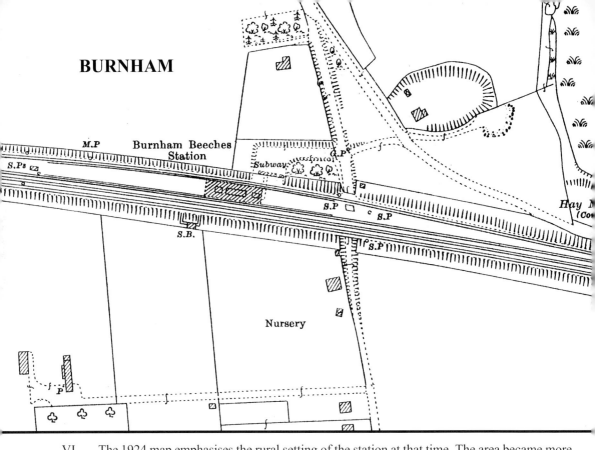

BURNHAM

M.P   Burnham Beeches
Station

Subway

Nursery

S.Ps

S.B.

S.P   S.P

S.P

S.P

Hay M
(Co

P

VI.   The 1924 map emphasises the rural setting of the station at that time. The area became more urbanised after World War II, but the population was only a little over 16,000 by 1960.

14.   The station opened in July 1899 and was provided with an island platform on the relief lines, an arrangement that remains unchanged. Burnham Beeches was an area of about 600 acres of "picturesque" woodland purchased by the City of London in 1879. (Lens of Sutton)

15.   No. 6846 *Ruckley Grange* waits to restart a down local train on 4th April 1959. The 27-lever box was in use until 19th November 1962. The station was closed as a wartime economy measure from April 1917 until March 1919. (B.W.Leslie)

16.   Burnham Beeches became Burnham (Bucks) on 1st September 1930, but the suffix was dropped on 5th May 1975, although Burnham-on-Sea had closed in 1951. The subway forms an unimpressive entrance and was photographed in 1997. (F.Hornby)

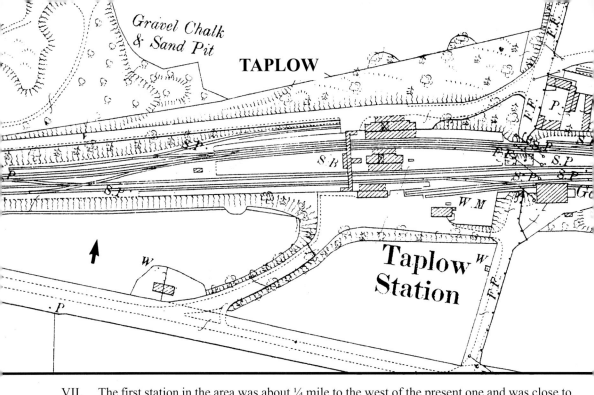

Gravel Chalk
& Sand Pit

TAPLOW

Taplow
Station

VII.   The first station in the area was about ¼ mile to the west of the present one and was close to the point where the line passes over the London-Bath road. It was a terminus for its first 13 months and was named "Maidenhead" until August 1854, when it became "Maidenhead and Taplow". A separate station for each place, almost two miles apart, came into use on 1st November 1871 and the original one was closed. This is the 1899 survey and it includes two signal boxes. The quadruple

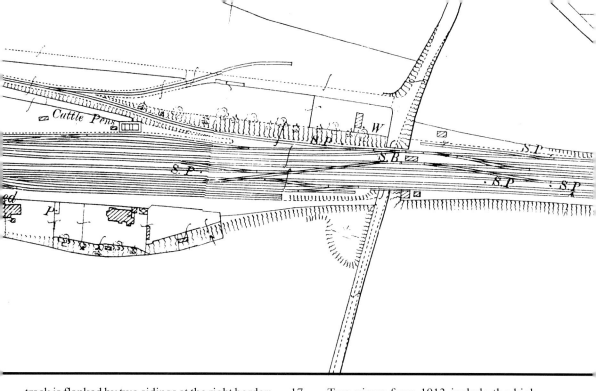

track is flanked by two sidings at the right border; the upper one ran to a tip. There was a branch from it to Geest's banana store from 1961 to 1973. Diagonally lower left is the Bath Road (A4 from 1919).

17.   Two views from 1913 include the high level West Box, which had a convenient entry from the footbridge to the machine room. Looking west, we see the relief lines of 1884 and the platforms for local trains. (LGRP/NRM)

18.   A down express passes the goods shed which was on the south side of the line, although the village was to the north. More importantly, it was close to the Bath Road. The two signal boxes were replaced by one on 30th June 1930. (LGRP/NRM)

19.   The 1930 box was situated at the east end of the island platform and was in use until 20th July 1974, although only as a ground frame after 1963. Equipped with 71 levers, it can be seen on the left as no. 5094 *Tretower Castle* speeds towards South Wales with the 1.55pm from Paddington on 20th June 1959. (H.C.Casserley)

20.   The infant Great Western Society established a store in the recently closed goods yard in 1966. No. 6106 was in steam on 17th September of that year on the occasion of a railtour from Birmingham hauled by no. 7808 *Cookham Manor*. On site were diesels nos D1030 and D837, together with no. 4079 *Pendennis Castle*. The Didcot site was available by the end of 1967 and the stock was moved there soon after. (S.C.Nash)

21.   The valencing was outstanding and the continuous arches were intended to give the impression of a colonnade. Although little used, the bridge to the down main platform was retained, complete with the GWR monograms. A speeding HST was recorded on 3rd September 1984. (M.J.Stretton)

22.   A long train of empty stone hoppers returns to Westbury, hauled by ARC's no. 59104 on 13th April 1994. The crossovers in this vicinity had been removed in the late 1950s and all the sidings had been lifted by 1974. (M.Turvey)

23.   Seen on the same day is one of the Thames Turbo units, a type introduced in 1992. Only this side of the building retained a canopy. The curves on the relief lines were slewed up to 10ft in 1978 to increase the line speed from 45 to 75 mph. (M.Turvey)

24.   Some of the sequences for the film "Chariots of Fire" were shot at this station in June 1980. The main building was erected on the up side and was photographed in 1994. The buildings on the down main line platform were demolished in May 1982. (F.Hornby)

EAST OF MAIDENHEAD

25.   As described, the first Maidenhead station was east of the Thames, close to the Bath Road to give easy access for those travelling by road from the west. Sadly we have found no plans of the layout, only this drawing which is not orientated. (British Rail)

26.   Brunel designed a two-span brick bridge to carry the line over the river. The exceptionally flat arches were ridiculed by the sceptics, but they arc still standing and carrying a heavier traffic than intended. The wooden centres are seen during construction; they were moved down a short distance following completion, in case the critics were correct. The bridge was widened on both sides in 1882, using the same design. (Railway Magazine)

VIII. The longitudinal section is from an original by Brunel.

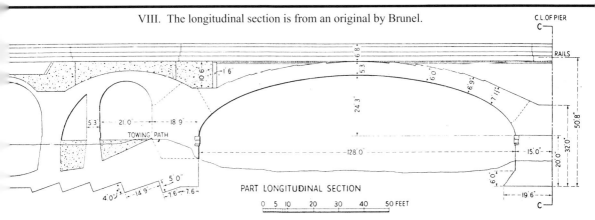

C.L.OF PIER

PART LONGITUDINAL SECTION

0 5 10   20   30   40   50 FEET

27. An equally innovative engineering scheme was successfully completed in 1999, when a flood relief tunnel was pushed bodily under the quadruple track, without interrupting train services. The 36 hydraulic jacks are concealed under boards in the foreground and exerted a thrust of 6000 tonnes. The ground under the track in the background was frozen during the operation. (E.Nuttall)

IX. At 23m wide, 9.5m high and 50m long, the concrete tube was the largest jacked structure in the world. It was thrust against a massive concrete block and the embankment was cut away from inside the box as it progressed under the tracks, which settled only 65mm. The Anti-Drag System (ADS) consisted of a membrane of heavily greased steel ropes, above and below the box, fluids being used on the walls to reduce friction.

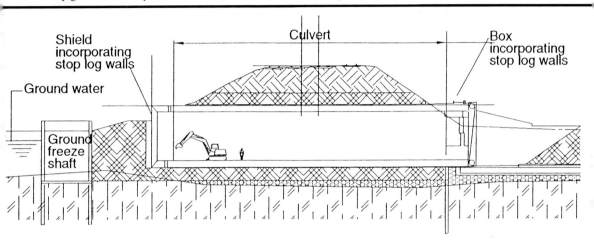

Longitudinal section on completion of tunnelling

0   5m 10m
Scale

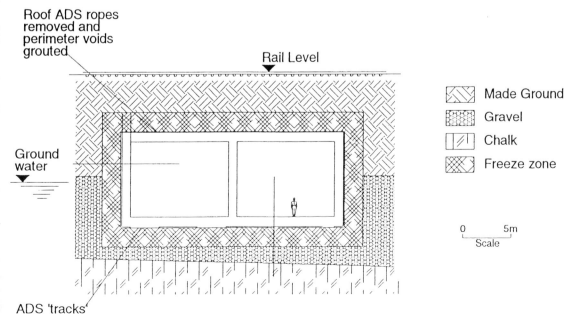

Cross section through culvert on completion of tunnelling

MAIDENHEAD

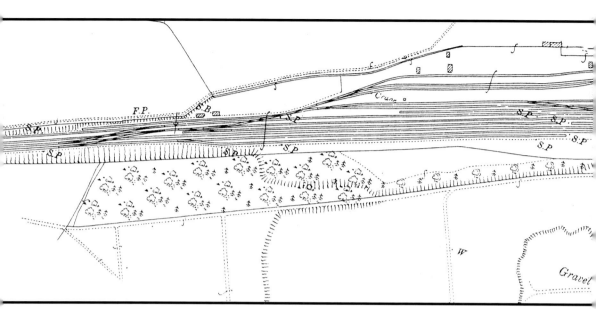

X.   The 1899 revision has been reduced to 17.5ins to 1 mile to show the full extent of the goods yard and both signal boxes. A new East Box was erected between the two pairs of tracks in 1923. A private siding for Cox Bros. Timber Yard was laid north of West Box by 1909. The crane shown was of 6-ton capacity. At the top is the branch to High Wycombe and Marlow.

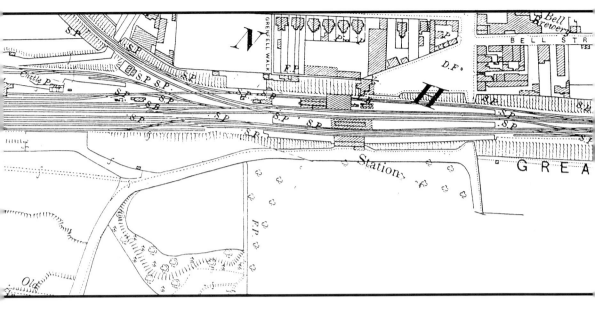

28.   A westward panorama from 1919 includes all five platforms and the roof over the branch track on the right. Opened on 1st November 1871, the station was close to the town centre. (LGRP/NRM)

29.   A closer view of the junction for High Wycombe includes the down refuge siding and Middle Box. Its predecessor is in the shadow of the water tank. The population of the town doubled from about 4000 during the second half of the 19th century. (LGRP/NRM)

30.   Seen in about 1930 is an up goods train on the main line. Such slow trains were commonly relegated to the relief lines, which had come into use here in 1893. (Stations UK)

31.   0-6-0PT no. 9463 takes water while standing on the down relief line as admirers discuss matters with the crew. Others relax on the seat with the guard of the two-wagon train. The roof extension over platform 5 is evident. (Lens of Sutton)

32.   No. 6973 *Bricklehampton Hall* is about to leave platform 1 with the 12.33pm Paddington to Reading on Sunday 16th February 1958. The close proximity of its cylinder to the platform is apparent; it was this factor that restricted the use of this class outside the Western Region. (B.W.Leslie)

33.   West, Middle and East boxes (53, 59 & 45 levers) were all closed on 8th December 1963 to be replaced by this box, which only lasted until 21st October 1974. The roof had failed when photographed in December 1972. The goods yard had closed on 19th July 1965. (J.C.Gillham)

34.   One siding was retained for use by the Ford Motor Company. Having discharged its load of cars there, a train of carflats passes through platform 4 on 1st March 1979, hauled by no. 37259. (G.Gillham)

35.　　More freight was photographed on the up relief line, this time
oil bound for London behind no.
60021 *Pen-y-Ghent* on 13th August
1994. The Marlow branch is on the
right; the sidings were disused by that
time. The one on the left had been
part of a loop until 1963. (M.Turvey)

36.　　The train shed was once a
fairly common feature of GWR
stations, but few others remain today.
This example protects the elevated
platforms from the cold north wind.
Unusually in two-car formation, no.
166215 was working the Marlow
service on 13th April 1994.
(M.Turvey)

37.   Generous shelter was provided for those using road transport and two subways were available, although one did not extend to platform 1. The barred windows on the right indicate that it is the ticket office. (V.Mitchell)

38.   A second view from July 2000 shows the unusual arrangement of platform 1, which was then little used. The new section is partially on the bridge over the main road; this structure was completely rebuilt in 1984. Passengers walk between the fences to the stairway. (V.Mitchell)

WEST OF MAIDENHEAD

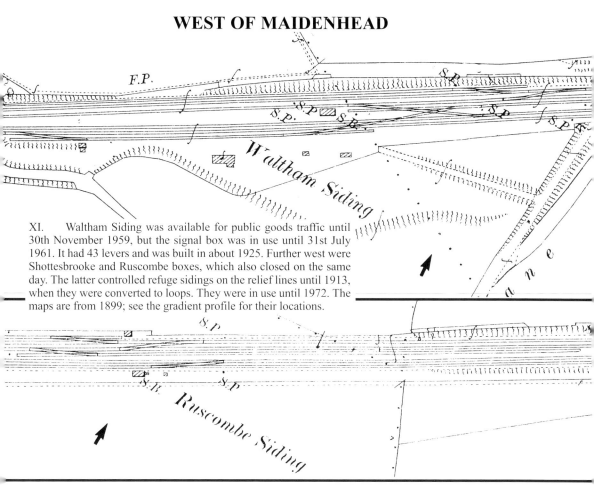

F.P.

Waltham Siding

XI.   Waltham Siding was available for public goods traffic until 30th November 1959, but the signal box was in use until 31st July 1961. It had 43 levers and was built in about 1925. Further west were Shottesbrooke and Ruscombe boxes, which also closed on the same day. The latter controlled refuge sidings on the relief lines until 1913, when they were converted to loops. They were in use until 1972. The maps are from 1899; see the gradient profile for their locations.

Ruscombe Siding

39.   Approaching Twyford on 12th October 1985 is no. 47345, with containers from Ripple Lane (Barking) bound for Southampton. The relief lines have carried a vast variety of merchandise, coal being the main commodity for several generations. (A.Dasi-Sutton)

TWYFORD

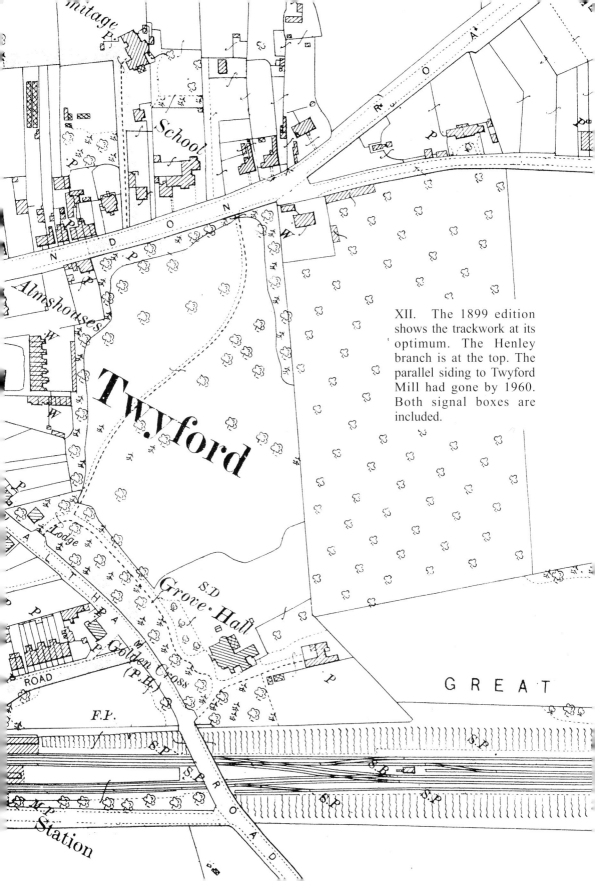

XII. The 1899 edition shows the trackwork at its optimum. The Henley branch is at the top. The parallel siding to Twyford Mill had gone by 1960. Both signal boxes are included.

School

Twyford

Almshouses

Lodge

Grove·Hall

S.D

Golden Cross
(P.H.)

GREAT

ROAD

Station

F.P.

ROAD

M.P.

40.   The first buildings were temporary and lasted until about 1845, when they were replaced by these. Note the early forms of signalling. The route was supplied with electric telegraph from the outset. (British Rail)

41.   The complexity of the approach to a dual gauge siding is evident as a down express approaches shortly before the conversion. On the right is the centring for the new bridge to carry Waltham Road over the main lines. The difference in the span of the two bridges is clearer in picture 45. (Locomotive Publishing Co.)

42.   New buildings were provided throughout at the time of the quadrupling in 1893. A local up train was recorded from the road bridge, with a "County" class 4-4-2T and a milk van leading. (Lens of Sutton)

43.   Departing with an up local train of compartment stock on 7th May 1955 is no. 6974 *Bryngwyn Hall*. Passengers were "requested", but not ordered, to use the bridge in those days. The population of Twyford was about 2200 at that time. (R.C.Riley)

44.   At the other end of the station, we witness the arrival of 2-6-2T no. 6130 on 1st June 1957. The curved platform is on the Henley branch. No. 4943 *Marrington Hall* is about to pass West Box. The goods yard had a 6-ton crane and closed on 7th September 1964. (A.E.Bennett)

45.   No. 6861 *Crynant Grange* has just passed over the crossovers, which were in use until 1961. A facing crossover on the relief lines only was added in 1972 to allow down Henley trains access to platform 4. East Box is evident; both were replaced by one in the fork of the junction on 23rd October 1961. It lasted until 20th March 1972. (Lens of Sutton)

46.   A small dock (left) was provided, its track being linked to that in the bay by a crossover until 1961. DMU no. L401 was working the 14.32 Henley service on 11th August 1980. (D.H.Mitchell)

47.   The curved platform on the Henley branch is evident as the 10.12 Reading to Paddington departs on 18th April 1992. The unusual formation is two "Bubblecars" with a trailer. New lights were provided and other improvements were made in 1989. (P.G.Barnes)

48.   The south side is seen in July 2000, by which time this platform was little used. However, there was a regular service at that time (outside peak hours) between Reading and Henley-on-Thames, reversing at this station. (V.Mitchell)

EAST OF READING

49.   To maintain a gentle gradient for the frail locomotives of the day, Brunel specified a two-mile long cutting at Sonning, up to 60ft deep. To widen it for quadruple track would have been very costly, thus its depth was simply reduced to increase floor width and retaining walls were built. The experimental single chimney "King", no. 6003 *King George IV*, passes under the lofty Bath Road bridge on 7th July 1956. (R.C.Riley)

Work-
shop | Offices | Turbine Hall

Boiler House

Loco
Shed

Wagon Tippler

Coal
Stocks

Weighbridge

BR (WR)

←———

50.   Entering Sonning Cutting from the west on 26th April 1973 is no. 5528 (later no. 31110) with correct headcodes for a Swindon-Old Oak Common van train. Beyond the rear vehicles were five sidings, laid down in 1941 for coal traffic. Earley Power Station sidings diverged from the headshunt. Sonning Sidings Box closed on 13th February 1961, as did Kennet Bridge Box, nearer to Reading. They had 54 and 8 levers respectively. (G.Gillham)

51.   Earley Power Station was constructed in 1942-46 and received an 0-4-0ST from Robert Stephenson & Hawthorn in each of those years. No. 1 was photographed near the main gate in October 1968. They were joined and eventually superseded by two diesel locomotives. (J.B.Horne)

←———

XIII.   The diagram shows the layout in 1950. The power station closed in 1976 and was largely demolished in 1983.

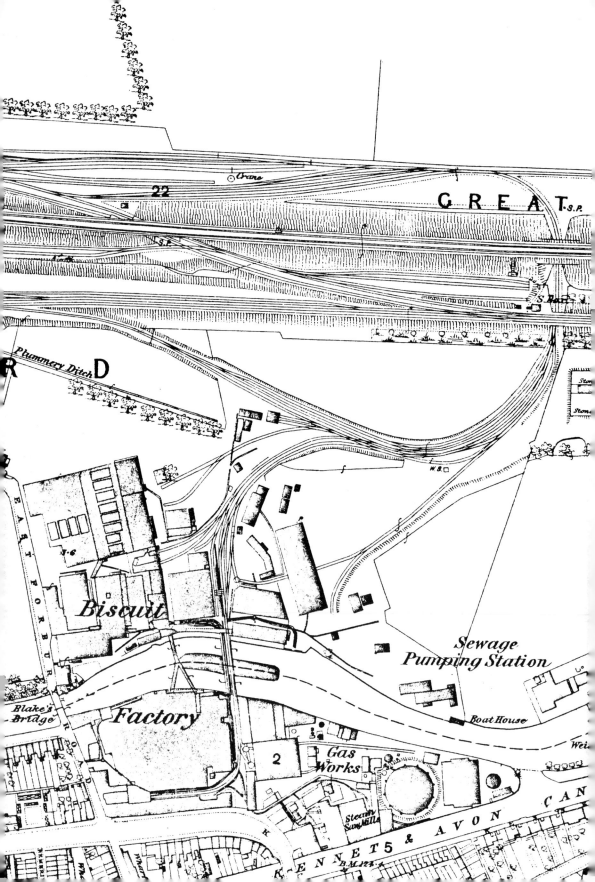

22

Crane

G R E A T. S.P.

S Post

Plummery Ditch

R D

Biscuit

EAST PORBURY ROAD

Factory

Blake's Bridge

2

Gas Works

Steam Saw Mills

W.B.

Sewage Pumping Station

Boat House

Weir

K E N N E T 5 & A V O N C A N

B.M.121.4

XIV. Huntley & Palmer's biscuit factory is seen on the 1879 survey. The double tracks across the page are those of the SER (lower) and the GWR. To facilitate the delivery of grain, the business was established at the confluence of two rivers and adjacent to the two railways mentioned, numerous roads and the canal. Sidings are shown from both companies' lines and the 1858 skew connection between them is also marked. Biscuit production ceased in 1977, it having started on this site in 1846. The firm purchased its first locomotives in 1875, two 0-4-0STs from Black, Hawthorn & Co., and in 1880 it despatched 16,500 tons of biscuits. Two more 0-4-0STs came from Pecketts in 1900. The 1913 layout can be seen in *Reading to Guildford*. Reading's second gasworks is shown; initially all its coal arrived by water. The third works was built further east and is marked on the next map. It was supplied by both railway companies, but the stockyard was north of the GWR on Kings Meadow. Transfer trains were run until 1966. Reading Gas Company bought a Hibberd diesel locomotive for internal use in 1947 and its successor, Southern Gas Board, purchased two Fowler diesels new in 1952. They were used at the naphtha storage tank farm built on Kings Meadow in the mid-1960s, when that fuel replaced coal for gas production.

52.   This is one of two fireless locomotives purchased from Bagnall in 1932. They ran until 1970, when the Southern Region connection was severed. The line under the Southern to the Western Region is seen in 1967; it was last used in March 1965. (J.B.Horne)

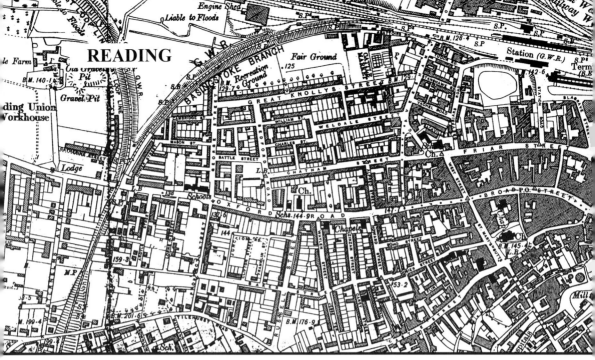

XV.   The 1900 edition at 6ins to 1 mile has the GWR station left of centre and the SER terminus is shown nearby. However, it was operated by the SECR from 1899 and the SR after 1923. That line curves away on the right, while the Newbury route is shown lower left. The GWR engine shed is near the divergence of the main lines on the left page. The Works marked north of the stations was

53.   As at Slough and elsewhere, the first passengers were confronted with up and down stations separated by a goods depot, all being on a loop on the town side of the main lines. Goods traffic was moved to a site north of the running lines in 1861 and the platforms were joined together. Separate platforms for standard gauge trains were also provided at this time. London-bound, *Hero* enters the eastern station, while another locomotive stands outside the original engine shed. The drawing was produced by Measom in 1852. (British Rail)

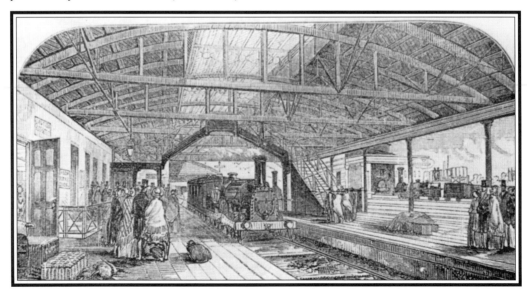

mainly concerned with signalling. The lack of detail of the GWR station was due to extensive site clearance at the time of the survey. This was in preparation for the construction of the present platforms. The confluence of the Rivers Thames and Kennet is above the bridges on the right page.

54.   Platform 4 is in the distance as no. 4082 *Windsor Castle* passes the 115-lever Main Line East Box on 1st April 1933, while hauling the LNER Royal Train. The lines on the left linked the SR and GWR and were in use from 1899 to 1965; they were known as West Incline. Middle Box had 21 levers and closed on 6th June 1959, but is not visible. (H.C.Casserley)

55.   The signalman's view from the box seen in picture 54 includes platforms 4 and 5 on the left. No. 6029 *King Edward VIII* is departing for Paddington, while freight passes through and a local train stands at

56.   Following nationalisation, a series of locomotive exchanges took place during performance trials in May 1948. Ex-LMS no. 46162 *Queen's Westminster Rifleman* was recorded at platform 5, while a GWR style diesel railcar waits to work a stopping service to Paddington. SR-built coaches stand at the ex-SER terminus on the left. (LGRP/NRM)

platform 9. The line on the right leads to Vastern Road Yard, which had 28 goods sidings at its peak. (P.Ransome Wallis/NRM)

57.   Arriving at platform 4 on 1st August 1959 is no. 4706 with the 1.25pm Paddington to Kingswear. The signal box (right), mentioned in captions 54 and 55, closed on 26th April 1965. The siding was removed soon after, to make way for the platform featured in the next view. (R.C.Riley)

58.   Platform 4a came into use on 6th September 1965, enabling the valuable former SR station site to be vacated. Operating difficulties resulted from Waterloo and Guildford services sharing one platform and so an additional face was provided on the left from 4th May 1975. The term "General" was in use from 26th September 1949 to 6th May 1973. (Lens of Sutton)

59.   Local trains to London have regularly used the bay numbered 6, which is between 5 and 8, while Henley-on-Thames trains frequent platform 10, the bay on the north side. No. 7 is the west end bay and is usually used by stopping trains to Oxford. No. 51408 is nearest and was nearing the end of its life when photographed on 11th November 1992. (M.J.Stretton)

60.   No. 47812 is approaching the west end of platform 8 on 25th May 1996 with the 06.34 Poole to Glasgow, the rear of the train still being on the east curve of the triangular junction. The locomotive will run round its train, using the centre road, before proceeding north. (P.G.Barnes)

61.   An eastward view on 8th November 1998 from the signal seen on the right of the previous picture has, from left to right, the up and down goods lines, a DMU at platform 9, Middle Road, an HST at platform 8, bay 6, platform 5, Up Main, and platforms 4 to 1. All except the goods lines are signalled for reversible running, the Reading Area Signalling Centre (opened April 1965) being near the left end of the footbridge. Platform 3 was used by one train per week in early 2000, the 07.20 Saturdays only to Bedwyn. (M.J.Stretton)

62.   Turning round on the same day we see the junction of the main lines, with the diesel depot in the fork and major engineering work in progress. The carriage siding on the left had not been used since 1970. Main Line West Box had 222 levers and was situated on the left from about 1896 to 1965. (M.J.Stretton)

63.   A further engineers occupation was recorded
on 10th January 1999 when work was in progress
between platforms 4 and 5. On the left are the
electrified lines at platforms 4a and 4b, while in the
background is the spacious footbridge which was
opened in 1988 to supplement the gloomy subway.
(M.J.Stretton)

64.   On the same day but looking east, we see the
former SER lines on the right and a class 165 DMU, a
type introduced on the Gatwick Airport services in
November 1993. In the background is the connection
between the two routes, known as East Incline. The
first such link passed through a tunnel under the GWR
main lines, just behind the camera, and then passed
an extensive goods yard. (M.J.Stretton)

65.   The Italianate-style building was erected on the site of the original down station and completed in 1868. It was supplanted by a new structure to the right, which was opened by Queen Elizabeth II on 4th April 1989. The old building later housed licensed bars, with doors on both north and south elevations. (V.Mitchell)

Platform changes

1899	1955
1 (dn.main)	4
1 West Bay	3
2 (bay)	2
3 (bay)	1
4 (centre)	5
5 (island)	8
4 East Bay	6
4 West Bay	7
6 (up relief)	9
6 East Bay	10

**Other Middleton Press albums
to feature Reading:**
Reading to Basingstoke
Reading to Guildford
Reading Tramways
Reading Trolleybuses

---

66.   The folly of the continental "open station" concept became apparent after the loss of millions of pounds and ticket barriers were reintroduced on 9th February 2000. However, there had to be a ticket inspector at the platform doors of "The Three Guineas" full time. Escalators are provided at the south end of the bridge and on platforms 5/8. (V.Mitchell)

Route connection alterations

Connection	Opened	Closed
Skew tunnel	1-12-1858	30-4-1979
West Incline	17-12-1899	4-4-1965
East Incline	16-3-1941*	In use
*Partial usage. Completed 25-5-1941.		

READING SHED

67.   The first engine shed was established in about 1840 and was glimpsed in picture no. 53. It was replaced by one in the triangular junction at an unknown date, 20 or 30 years later. It had a central turntable with radiating tracks. Eventually, there were 20 lines in enlarged buildings. This is the east end prior to 1930, when the internal turntable was removed. (British Rail)

68.   Nine through roads were provided in 1930 and a new 65ft. turntable was installed outside the west end in 1925. This is the east end during World War II, when some LMS engines were present. A three-road shed for DMU servicing was added in 1959 and extended in 1964. Steam operation ceased here on 2nd January 1965. The lifting shop is on the right. (British Rail)

69.   The depot was developed further in the early 1990s for the third generation of diesels, the Turbos. Two photographs from a Newbury-bound train in July 2000 show its extent. This westward view includes the EWS locomotive servicing shed in front of the two larger ones used for Thames Trains. The area on the right was first used for permanent way material in 1972. The steam shed had stood in the centre of this panorama. (V.Mitchell)

70.   A northward view has West Curve (originally West Loop) on the left and the Turbo lavatory flushing apron beyond the buffers. There had been no access to the steam depot from this direction, the ground being marshy. A tip siding was laid in about 1900 and eventually seven carriage sidings were sited here. Two were later used for fuelling DMUs; there were 19 sidings south of the depot in 2000. (V.Mitchell)

READING WEST

71.   The station opened on 1st July 1906 and offered further travel improvements to the local residents who had been given the luxury of electric trams in 1903. We look south and see the junction signals in the distance. (Stations UK)

72.   Looking in the other direction in 1920, the great length of the platforms becomes apparent. They were used by the long trains working between the South Coast and the Midlands via Oxford. (LGRP/NRM)

73.   Running south in August 1963 with vans is 2-6-2T no. 6107. At the rear of the train is Oxford Road Junction, named after the highway below it long before the station was thought of. (H.F.Wheeller)

74.   Passing over Oxford Road on 12th May 1964 is no. 34029 *Lundy* with the "Pines Express"; the train can be seen on the Reading West Curve. Southern Region locomotives worked to and from Oxford. (H.C.Casserley)

75.   Following the end of steam traction, most trains between the North and South reversed at Reading from 1966 onwards, thus these platforms could be reduced in length as they no longer stopped here. No. 50043 *Eagle* is bound for the West of England on 3rd April 1982. The oil tanks of the diesel depot are in the near background. (A.Dasi-Sutton)

**Pictures nos. 33 to 44 in our *Reading to Basingstoke*
album include a great variety of trains at this location.**

SOUTH OF READING WEST

76.   The goods lines are in the foreground in this northward view from 1919. The far line on the left was a refuge siding until 1963. The 25-lever Southcote Junction Box was just beyond the left border of the picture and was in use until 26th April 1965. (LGRP/NRM)

XVI.   Southcote Junction is the point of divergence of the Basingstoke and Berks & Hants lines (centre). The Coley branch to Reading Central Goods (opened 1908) is at the bottom of this 1932 survey. The branch is illustrated in *Reading to Basingstoke*, pictures 50-54.

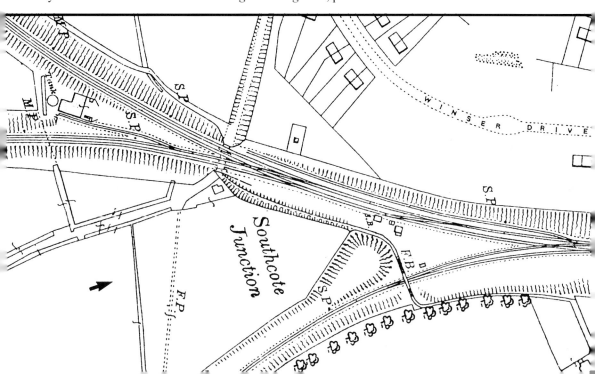

77.   No. 33029 is working a Southampton to Liverpool train on 29th April 1976 and is passing the junction of the remaining connection to the Reading Central single line. The other junction is near the rear of the train. Lower right are gas bottles for point heaters for the branch which closed on 5th December 1983. (G.Gillham)

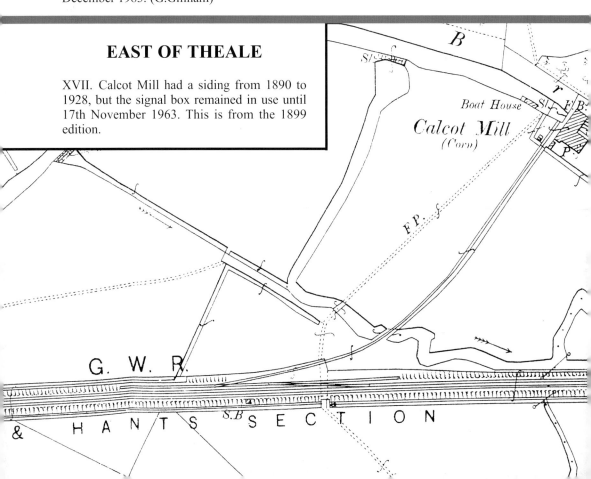

EAST OF THEALE

XVII. Calcot Mill had a siding from 1890 to 1928, but the signal box remained in use until 17th November 1963. This is from the 1899 edition.

B

Boat House

Calcot Mill
(Corn)

F.P.

G. W. R.

& HANTS S.B. SECTION

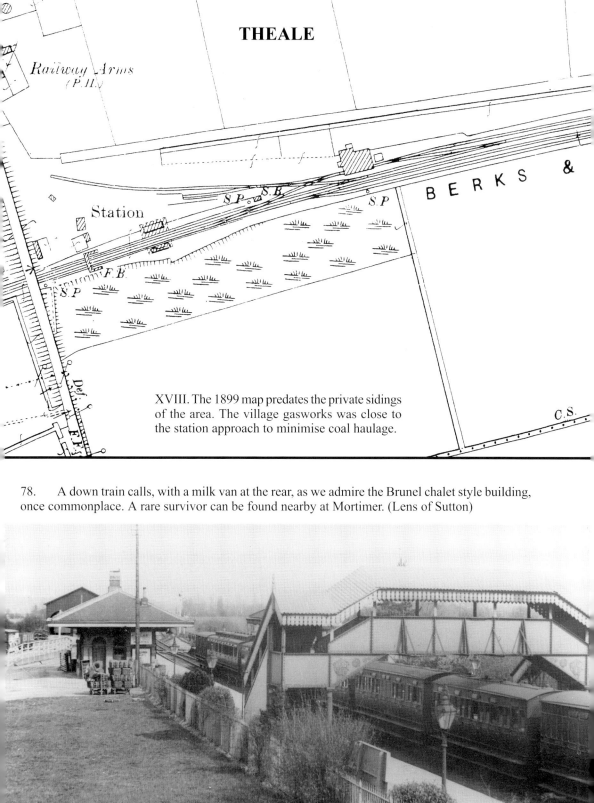

THEALE

'orks

Railway Arms
(P.H.)

Station

S.P. S.B.

S.P

BERKS &

S.P

F.B.

S.P

Def.

F.B.

C.S.

XVIII. The 1899 map predates the private sidings of the area. The village gasworks was close to the station approach to minimise coal haulage.

78. A down train calls, with a milk van at the rear, as we admire the Brunel chalet style building, once commonplace. A rare survivor can be found nearby at Mortimer. (Lens of Sutton)

79.   A poor postcard view from the footbridge includes the goods shed and the signal box. The latter was in use until September 1977, by which date a reversible goods line ran behind it. A private siding was provided beyond the goods shed in 1940 for Imperial Tobacco. It was used by Pressed Steel from 1952 to 1976. (Lens of Sutton)

80.   The Road Motor Department was based at Slough, but part of its open bodied fleet was assembled here for a photograph in 1934. Note the Foden steam overtype on the left. The GWR had been pioneers in this field. (M.W.Earley/NRM)

81.   No. 50002 speeds through with the 07.53 Paignton to Paddington on 14th May 1974, by which time the original buildings had vanished. There had been no staff since 2nd November 1964; the suffix "Halt" appeared in the timetables from 18th April 1966 to 5th May 1969. (G.Gillham)

82.   Local goods traffic ceased on 1st July 1970, but some private sidings had been established west of the station. Coal is destined to Padworth Sidings behind no. 37213 on 10th July 1990. The reversible goods line is in the distance. (J.S.Petley)

WEST OF
THEALE

83.   Approaching the line mentioned in the previous caption is no. 33047. The Blue Circle cement wagons are running from the depot in the left background to Northam, near Southampton, on 5th March 1983. The two sidings were laid in 1962 to serve four different firms. (G.Gillham)

84.   The western siding was used by Murco Petroleum from May 1970; their tanks are in the left background of this July 2000 picture. The area had previously been used for track materials. Foster Yeoman used the sidings on the left from January 1982. Blue Circle brought in cement from 1983 and ARC used the sidings at the east end of the complex, much of the stone being used for road making. (V.Mitchell)

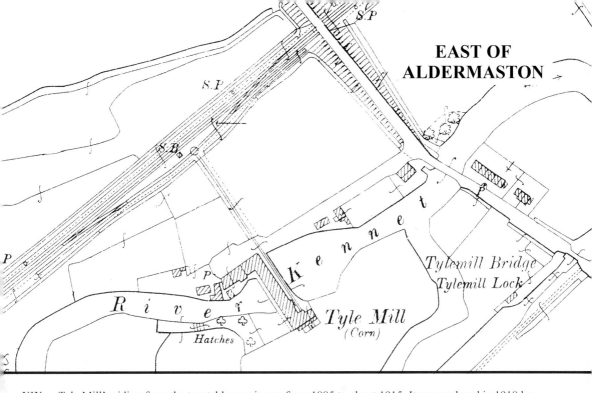

XIX.   Tyle Mill's siding from the turntable was in use from 1885 to about 1915. It was replaced in 1918 by two sidings parallel to the main line. These were used until 1937 and the signal box closed on 20th January 1938.

85.   Up and down goods lines were added for over one mile east of Aldermaston in 1943, as far as Ufton Crossing where a new signal box was built. The up one lasted until 1963, but part of the down track was duplicated in 1974. Class 52 no. 1054 *Western Governor* was in charge of the down "Cornish Riviera" on 14th May 1974. (G.Gillham)

86. The previous photograph was taken from the bridge in the left background, while this one is from the bridge at the end of the platforms. Since 1974, the single line has formed a headshunt for Padworth Sidings, right. The first was laid for the Ministry of Fuel and Power in 1942 and five others followed between 1954 and 1972. Users in 1983 were Conoco (oil), Goodwin (coal) and Foster Yeoman (stone). No. 50023 is destined for Penzance with the 13.02 from Paddington on 2nd September 1989. (P.G.Barnes)

2nd - SINGLE   SINGLE - 2nd

5724

Reading West to

Reading West   **THEALE**   Reading West
Theale   Theale

5724

(W)   1/4 Fare 1/4   (W)

For conditions see over   For conditions see over

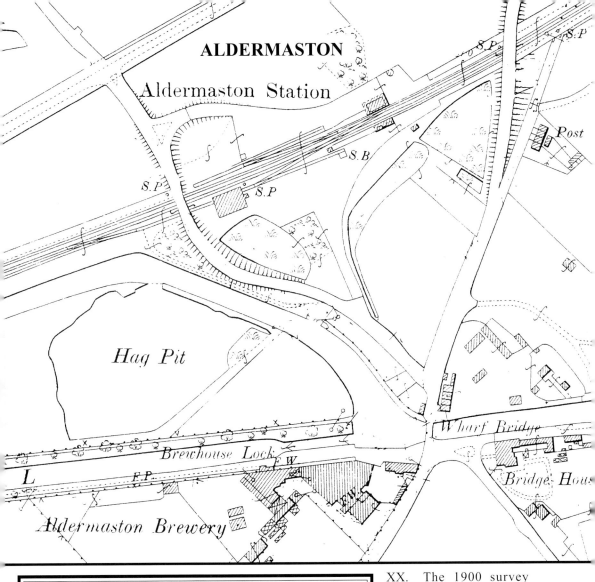

ALDERMASTON

Aldermaston Station

S.P

S.B

S.P   S.P

Post

Hag Pit

Wharf Bridge

Brewhouse Lock

Bridge House

L   F.P   W

Aldermaston Brewery

Aldermaston Station.

XX. The 1900 survey shows that the station was flanked by road bridges and that there was road access to both platforms.

87. A badly copied postcard reveals that the wayside station was provided with the Brunel chalet-style buildings, standard on the Berks & Hants route. A down train approaches under the composite iron and brick bridge. (Lens of Sutton)

88. An eastward view includes the station approach and the cattle dock. The latter, together with its associated siding, was removed in 1940. The population dropped from 783 in 1851 to 482 in 1901. (Lens of Sutton)

89. A westward panorama from about 1919 includes the signal box, which was replaced in 1920 by the one seen in the next picture. A 2-ton crane was provided, but goods facilities were withdrawn on 1st December 1965. (LGRP/NRM)

90.   The up platform (left) was extended and the shelter erected for wartime traffic in 1940. Part of the GWR headquarters was evacuated from Paddington to nearby Beenham Grange in 1939 and six steel-framed office buildings were erected subsequently. A number of changes took place on 31st March 1974: the crossover was taken out of use, as was the connection (under the bridge) to the down goods loop and the signal box was closed. (Lens of Sutton)

91.   A later look from about the same viewpoint reveals that the up platform had lost its extension. The headshunt passes under the brick arch. Staffing ceased on 2nd November 1964 and halt status followed, as at Theale. (Lens of Sutton)

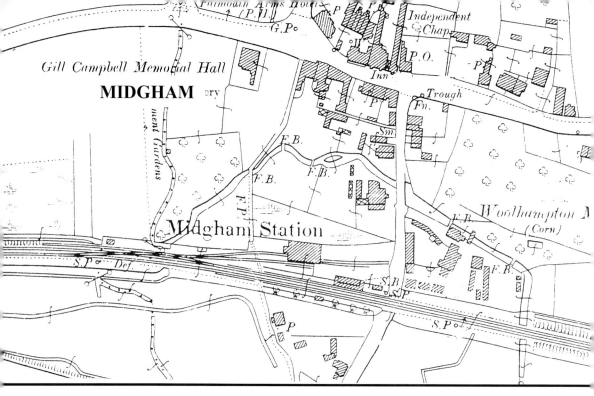

XXI. The station was named "Woolhampton" until 1st March 1873, at which date six trains called on weekdays and two on Sundays. The 1900 survey reveals the close proximity of the station to the centre of Woolhampton, which had a population of nearly 500 at that time, whereas remote Midgham was under 300.

92.   Fortunately station views were in demand by postcard purchasers and in this one we can see one of the wicket gates. These were closed for shorter periods than the main crossing gates and were of value to pedestrians in a hurry. This box was built in 1897. (Lens of Sutton)

93.   An eastward view in 1919 includes the goods shed and evidence of a substantial milk traffic. By that time there were ten weekday down trains, the 5.5pm from Paddington arriving at 6.15 with only one stop. (LGRP/NRM)

94.   Of the eleven down stopping trains, Mondays to Fridays in 1959, five were second class only autotrains, such as this example headed by 0-4-2T no. 1444. In the background is the connection to the goods yard, which had a 2-ton crane and closed on 1st August 1960. (Lens of Sutton)

95.   Douai School is mentioned under the running-in board. This refers to a French college that moved nearby prior to World War I. The "Cornish Riviera" rushes past the WWII up platform shelter extension in 1961, with another "Warship" in charge. The wartime platform canopy was of benefit to headquarters staff using Hyde End House, Wasing Place and Wharf House as temporary offices. (Stations UK)

96.   Destaffing and halt status dates are as for Theale. The signal box remained in use until 5th December 1977, it having controlled full lifting barriers since August 1974. They were worked from Colthrop Crossing Box (two miles west) subsequently. The old shelter on the left was still in use in 2000. (Lens of Sutton)

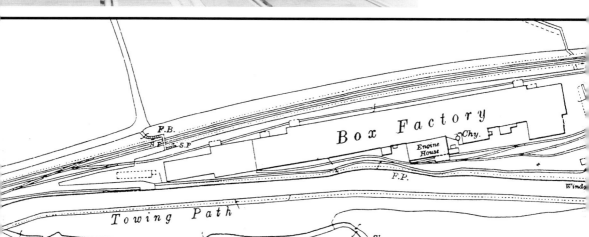

WEST OF MIDGHAM

97.   At Colthrop, a large paper and board mill complex grew up on both sides of the line, connected by a busy level crossing. When the 1978 resignalling was introduced the former Colthrop siding signal box was retained to supervise this, and also the nearby crossings at Thatcham and Midgham, by closed-circuit television. With the North Mill in the background, class 117 DMU no. L413 forms the 12.15 Bedwyn to Reading on 5th March 1985. The two sidings in the background were laid for a Naval Depot during WWII. The sidings on the down side were in use from 1912 to 1971. The box was repainted in GWR colours (also double glazed) in time for its centenary in 1999. (G.Gillham)

XXII.   Colthrop Box is on the right page of this 1932 map, which is at 20ins to 1 mile. The Kennet & Avon Canal is parallel to the southern boundary of the works and Thatcham station is just beyond the left border.

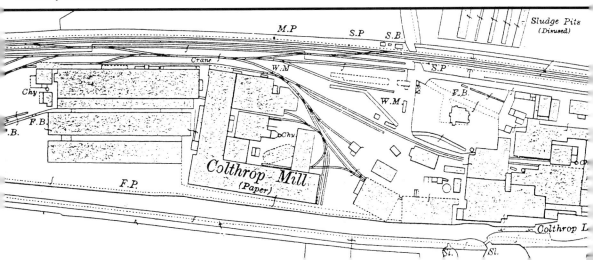

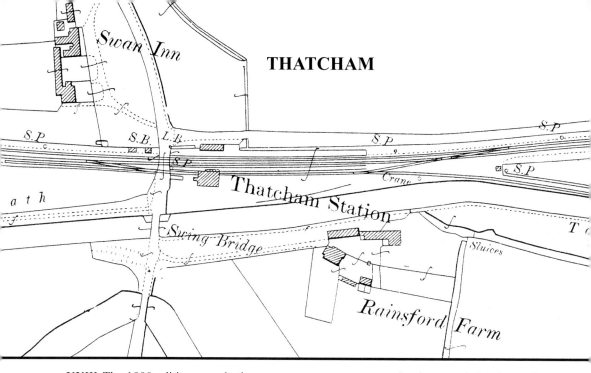

THATCHAM

XXIII. The 1900 edition reveals the uncommon arrangement of a three-track level crossing on a double track railway. The goods line lasted until 1967. The station served a community of nearly 6000 people at the time of the map.

98.   The 2-ton crane is visible in this 1919 view, together with a notice about curtailment of services due to the war. Nevertheless, there were nine down trains calling on weekdays. The RCH poster is on the end of the tiny down side shelter. (LGRP/NRM)

99. Looking along the up platform we see the southern part of the board mills of Reeds Cartons Ltd. There was a connection from their sidings to the down line, near the water tank, from 1922 to about 1959. The extra shelter was used by goods clerks evacuated to Crookham House during World War II. (Lens of Sutton)

100. The local population had risen to 7500 by 1961, but nevertheless the station was soon destaffed, demolished, relegated to a halt and deprived of goods traffic. (Dates as for Theale). This is a westward view prior to the demolition of the 1921 box in 1976. Further west, Thatcham West Box controlled entry to the up goods loop and a massive ordnance depot from 1940 to 1966. (Lens of Sutton)

101. A class 101 DMU passes over the level crossing on 5th December 1990, while working from Bedwyn to Reading. The barriers are controlled under CCTV from Colthrop Crossing box. The points to the Army siding are near the rear of the train. New shelters and a ticket office were erected, the latter being officially opened on 8th August 1987. (M.Turvey)

NEWBURY RACECOURSE

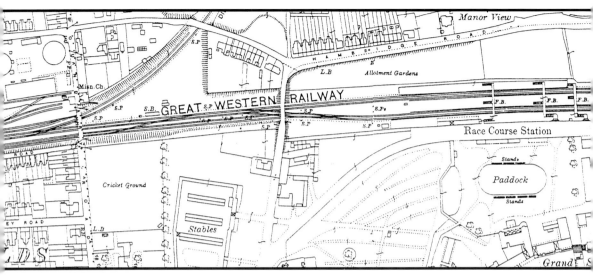

XXIV. The 1932 map is at 15ins to 1 mile to show the great extent of this station. Its signal box is on the right page, while Newbury East Junction Box is on the left one, as is the line from Didcot. This box opened in 1910 and closed on 20th March 1978, although the Didcot line had ceased to be used in 1962.

102.	An eastward panorama in 1919 has the main lines on the leflt. The station opened on 26th September 1905, but the loops rejoined the main lines in the foreground until 1910, when quadruple track was provided to Newbury station. (LGRP/NRM)

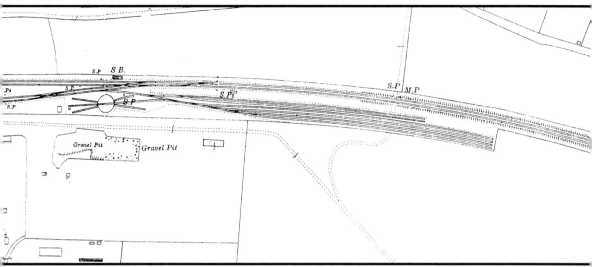

103.   Newbury Racecourse was requisitioned during World War I. The nearer footbridge seems to have been erected by the Army. It is not a GWR design and does not appear on OS maps. Many extra sidings were laid across the course to serve six massive sheds used for munitions. During the early part of the subsequent war, emergency offices were provided in withdrawn restaurant cars parked in the racetrain sidings. (Lens of Sutton)

104.   Newbury Racecourse Signal Box was at the east end of the loops and was in use until 16th January 1978. It is seen on 5th March 1960 as no. 6010 *King Charles I* is about to be turned, having worked the Members Special, an all first class train. (R.C.Riley)

105.   The box is behind the second coach of the 14.30 Paddington to Paignton, seen on 17th March 1973 behind no. D1652 (later no. 47068). The loops are on the right; access to them had been singled on 31st March 1968. There had been six carriage sidings in the right distance until November 1967. Two remained in place and long out of use in 2000. On the left are the white storage tanks of BP Oil, the sidings for which came into use in 1962. (G.Gillham)

106. The station was only open on race days until 1988; 6th January 1979 was not one of them. An up train from the West of England accelerates east behind its roaring class 47. There have been only three platforms since 1978. Local trains have called approximately hourly on weekdays since 3rd October 1988. (P.G.Barnes)

107. The remaining single loop line is in the left background as a Turbo makes a stop at platform 2 on 16th November 1996. No. 1 is in the middle, unusually, and it has had a reversible running line since 1978. Passenger access is through the industrial estate and the gate on the right; a new footbridge has been provided. (M.Turvey)

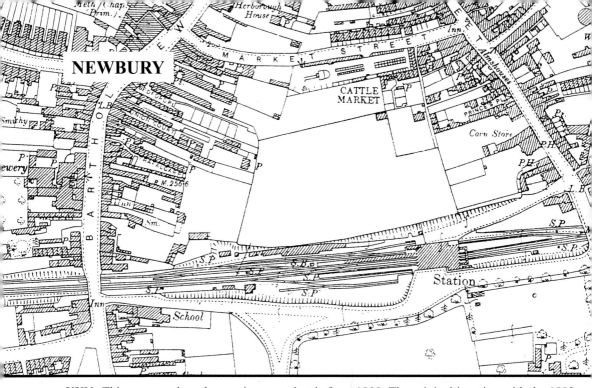

NEWBURY

XXV. This map overlaps the previous one, but is from 1900. The original junction with the 1882 Didcot line is shown, together with the first East Junction Box. The gasworks siding was in use until 1961.

108.   As shown on the map, the station had a roof over the tracks and only two through lines. The latter feature caused congestion with the advent of the Didcot-Southampton service and so plans were made for the provision of through lines. (Lens of Sutton)

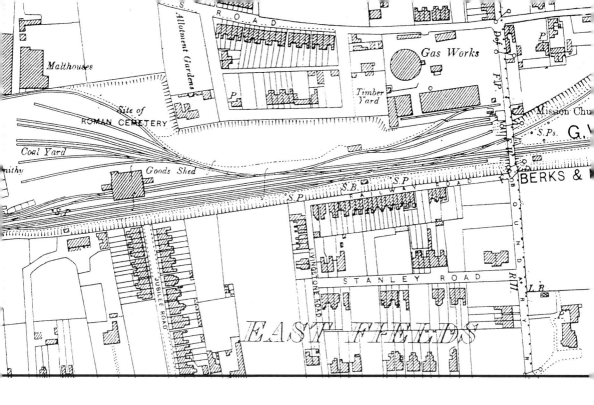

109.   The west of the station is seen with Newbery's container at Newbury. The material in the right foreground suggests that work is starting on the widening, which would date the view at about 1909. There had earlier been a turntable on the site. (Lens of Sutton)

110. The through tracks are seen soon after the completion of the new station in May 1910. The long bay on the right was often used for starting local trains to Reading. (LGRP/NRM)

111. Until the introduction of the 6100 class 2-6-2Ts in 1931, many local services were operated by 4-4-2Ts. The bay in which the spare coach is standing was also used for trains starting for Didcot. (Lens of Sutton)

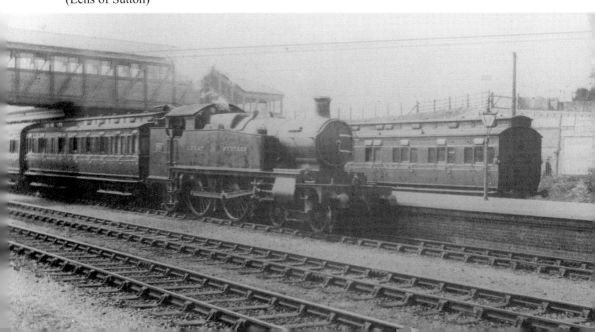

112.   Of the 38 diesel railcars built by the GWR, the final four were designed to work with an ordinary 70ft. corridor coach between a pair of them. These are working a down local train from Reading on 2nd September 1953. (D.B.Clayton)

Other views of this station can be seen in our *Didcot to Winchester* album.

113.   A view towards London on the same day includes the 1910 road bridge, the extended goods shed and Middle Box, which closed at the same time as its neighbours. The crossovers were taken out of use at that time as well. The 4300 class often appeared on Didcot trains. (D.B.Clayton)

Gt. Western Ry   Gt. Western Ry
WOODHAY   WOODHAY
                TO
            NEWBURY
          THIRD CLASS
          7d C Fare 7d C
Newbury   Newbury
FOR CONDITIONS SEE BACK W.H

5960

114.   Former LSWR engines were used in the final years of the Didcot-Winchester route. Working the 2.56pm Oxford to Southampton Terminus on 12th March 1955 was class T9 4-4-0 no. 30117. (S.C.Nash)

115.   The down side buildings were recorded on 6th June 1957, along with a Royal Mail van. The site of the down bay on the left became a car park. (R.M.Casserley)

116.   The bay on the left was used by Lambourn trains until their withdrawal in January 1960, while the one on the right often accommodated Winchester services, until they were withdrawn in March 1960. The coaches on the right are in a parallel berthing siding; beyond it was the horse dock siding. (Lens of Sutton)

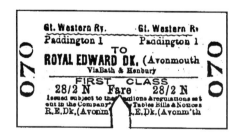

117.   No. D1022 *Western Sentinel* is about to restart the 08.35 Penzance to Paddington on 17th February 1973. Mk II coaches, new rail for the down loop and electric platform lighting were all welcome signs of improvement. (G.Gillham)

118. The track was simplified with the introduction of colour light signals in 1978, these being controlled from Reading. A van train has been held on the through line as a DMU departs for Reading on 9th June 1984. Lower left is the "Down Passenger Loop" from Newbury Racecourse, the track having been seen earlier in picture no. 113. (P.G.Barnes)

⟶

119. Here is a typical scene from the 1980s. An HST races through on 24th December 1988, forming the 13.50 Paddington to Penzance, while a DMU waits to depart for Bedwyn at 14.31, a destination hourly at that period. (P.G.Barnes)

⟶

120. The class 166 Turbos represent the third generation of diesel cars on the route and by far the best yet. There were 13 trains terminating in the bay Mondays to Fridays in the Summer timetable for 2000, this being the 14.35 from Reading on 27th July. (V.Mitchell)

MP Middleton Press

Easebourne Lane, Midhurst, W Sussex. GU29 9AZ Tel: 01730 813169 Fax: 01730 812601
If books are not available from your local transport stockist, order direct with cheque,
Visa or Mastercard, post free UK.

BRANCH LINES
Branch Line to Allhallows
Branch Line to Alton
Branch Lines around Ascot
Branch Line to Ashburton
Branch Lines around Bodmin
Branch Line to Bude
Branch Lines around Canterbury
Branch Lines around Chard & Yeovil
Branch Lines around Cromer
Branch Lines to East Grinstead
Branch Lines of East London
Branch Lines to Effingham Junction
Branch Lines around Exmouth
Branch Line to Fairford
Branch Lines around Gosport
Branch Line to Hawkhurst
Branch Lines to Horsham
Branch Lines around Huntingdon
Branch Line to Ilfracombe
Branch Line to Kingswear
Branch Lines to Launceston & Princetown
Branch Lines to Longmoor
Branch Line to Looe
Branch Line to Lyme Regis
Branch Lines around March
Branch Lines around Midhurst
Branch Line to Minehead
Branch Line to Moretonhampstead
Branch Line to Padstow
Branch Lines around Plymouth
Branch Lines to Seaton and Sidmouth
Branch Line to Selsey
Branch Lines around Sheerness
Branch Line to Shrewsbury
Branch Line to Swanage *updated*
Branch Line to Tenterden
Branch Lines to Torrington
Branch Lines to Tunbridge Wells
Branch Line to Upwell
Branch Lines of West London
Branch Lines around Weymouth
Branch Lines around Wisbech

NARROW GAUGE BRANCH LINES
Branch Line to Lynton
Branch Lines around Portmadoc 1923-46
Branch Lines around Porthmadog 1954-94
Branch Line to Southwold
Douglas to Port Erin
Kent Narrow Gauge
Two-Foot Gauge Survivors
Romneyrail
Southern France Narrow Gauge
Vivarais Narrow Gauge

SOUTH COAST RAILWAYS
Ashford to Dover
Bournemouth to Weymouth
Brighton to Eastbourne
Brighton to Worthing
Dover to Ramsgate
Eastbourne to Hastings
Hastings to Ashford
Portsmouth to Southampton
Southampton to Bournemouth

SOUTHERN MAIN LINES
Basingstoke to Salisbury
Bromley South to Rochester
Crawley to Littlehampton
Dartford to Sittingbourne
East Croydon to Three Bridges
Epsom to Horsham
Exeter to Barnstaple
Exeter to Tavistock
Faversham to Dover

London Bridge to East Croydon
Orpington to Tonbridge
Tonbridge to Hastings
Salisbury to Yeovil
Swanley to Ashford
Tavistock to Plymouth
Victoria to East Croydon
Waterloo to Windsor
Waterloo to Woking
Woking to Portsmouth
Woking to Southampton
Yeovil to Exeter

EASTERN MAIN LINES
Fenchurch Street to Barking
Ipswich to Saxmundham
Liverpool Street to Ilford

WESTERN MAIN LINES
Ealing to Slough
Ely to Kings Lynn
Exeter to Newton Abbot
Paddington to Ealing
Slough to Newbury

COUNTRY RAILWAY ROUTES
Andover to Southampton
Bath Green Park to Bristol
Bath to Evercreech Junction
Bournemouth to Evercreech Jn.
Cheltenham to Andover
Croydon to East Grinstead
Didcot to Winchester
East Kent Light Railway
Fareham to Salisbury
Frome to Bristol
Guildford to Redhill
Reading to Basingstoke
Reading to Guildford
Redhill to Ashford
Salisbury to Westbury
Stratford upon Avon to Cheltenham
Strood to Paddock Wood
Taunton to Barnstaple
Wenford Bridge to Fowey
Westbury to Bath
Woking to Alton
Yeovil to Dorchester

GREAT RAILWAY ERAS
Ashford from Steam to Eurostar
Clapham Junction 50 years of change
Festiniog in the Fifties
Festiniog in the Sixties
Isle of Wight Lines 50 years of change
Railways to Victory 1944-46
SECR Centenary album
Talyllyn 50 years of change
Yeovil 50 years of change

LONDON SUBURBAN RAILWAYS
Caterham and Tattenham Corner
Charing Cross to Dartford
Clapham Jn. to Beckenham Jn.
Crystal Palace (HL) & Catford Loop
East London Line
Finsbury Park to Alexandra Palace
Kingston and Hounslow Loops
Lewisham to Dartford
Lines around Wimbledon
London Bridge to Addiscombe
Mitcham Junction Lines
North London Line
South London Line
West Croydon to Epsom
West London Line
Willesden Junction to Richmond
Wimbledon to Epsom

STEAMING THROUGH
Steaming through Cornwall
Steaming through the Isle of Wight
Steaming through Kent
Steaming through West Hants
Steaming through West Sussex

TRAMWAY CLASSICS
Aldgate & Stepney Tramways
Barnet & Finchley Tramways
Bath Tramways
Bournemouth & Poole Tramways
Brighton's Tramways
Burton & Ashby Tramways
Camberwell & W.Norwood Tramways
Clapham & Streatham Tramways
Croydon's Tramways
Dover's Tramways
East Ham & West Ham Tramways
Edgware and Willesden Tramways
Eltham & Woolwich Tramways
Embankment & Waterloo Tramways
Enfield & Wood Green Tramways
Exeter & Taunton Tramways
Greenwich & Dartford Tramways
Hammersmith & Hounslow Tramways
Hampstead & Highgate Tramways
Hastings Tramways
Holborn & Finsbury Tramways
Ilford & Barking Tramways
Kingston & Wimbledon Tramways
Lewisham & Catford Tramways
Liverpool Tramways 1. Eastern Routes
Liverpool Tramways 2. Southern Routes
Liverpool Tramways 3. Northern Routes
Maidstone & Chatham Tramways
Margate to Ramsgate
North Kent Tramways
Norwich Tramways
Portsmouth's Tramways
Reading Tramways
Seaton & Eastbourne Tramways
Shepherds Bush & Uxbridge Tramway
Southampton Tramways
Southend-on-sea Tramways
Southwark & Deptford Tramways
Stamford Hill Tramways
Twickenham & Kingston Tramways
Victoria & Lambeth Tramways
Waltham Cross & Edmonton Tramway
Walthamstow & Leyton Tramways
Wandsworth & Battersea Tramways

TROLLEYBUS CLASSICS
Croydon Trolleybuses
Bournemouth Trolleybuses
Hastings Trolleybuses
Maidstone Trolleybuses
Reading Trolleybuses
Woolwich & Dartford Trolleybuses

WATERWAY ALBUMS
Kent and East Sussex Waterways
London to Portsmouth Waterway
West Sussex Waterways

MILITARY BOOKS
Battle over Portsmouth
Battle over Sussex 1940
Blitz over Sussex 1941-42
Bombers over Sussex 1943-45
Bognor at War
Military Defence of West Sussex
Military Signals from the South Coast
Secret Sussex Resistance
Surrey Home Guard
Sussex Home Guard

OTHER RAILWAY BOOKS
Garraway Father & Son
Index to all Middleton Press stations
Industrial Railways of the South-East
South Eastern & Chatham Railways
London Chatham & Dover Railway
War on the Line (SR 1939-45)